PRESENTED TO:

_____

FROM:

_____

# THE GIFT OF CHRISTMAS

HEARTWARMING REFLECTIONS
ON THE MEANING
OF THE SEASON

ISBN 978-1-60587-535-4

Published by Freeman-Smith, a division of Worthy Media, Inc.,
134 Franklin Road, Suite 200, Brentwood, Tennessee 37027.

Cover Design by Kim Russell / Wahoo Designs
Page Layout by Bart Dawson

Printed in the United States of America

3 4 5—CHG—17 16 15 14 13

# THE GIFT OF CHRISTMAS

## HEARTWARMING REFLECTIONS ON THE MEANING OF THE SEASON

FREEMAN-SMITH

# TABLE OF CONTENTS

*But the angel said to them,
"Do not be afraid, for you see,
I announce to you good news of
great joy that will be for all
the people: because today in the
city of David was born for you
a Savior, who is Christ the Lord."*

Luke 2:10-11 HCSB

# INTRODUCTION

*C*hristmas is intended to be a joyful season, a time when we gather together to exchange gifts and celebrate God's ultimate gift to the world. Yet sometimes, amid the crush of holiday obligations, we may be tempted to forget, at least temporarily, the One whose birth we celebrate.

This book is intended to remind family members of all ages that God's promises are everlasting, that His joy is available to all, and that His grace is given freely to those who accept His Son into their hearts.

The Christmas holidays are, of course, a time when Christians the world over celebrate the birth of Jesus. Have you made the choice to rejoice? Hopefully so. After all, this holiday season, like each one before it, is a gift from God, a gift to be savored and celebrated. And, the best day to begin that celebration is the current one.

Christmas is based on
an exchange of gifts;
the gift of God to man, his Son;
and the gift of man to God,
when we first
give ourselves to God.

—

Vance Havner

# CHAPTER 1

# THE GIFT OF CHRISTMAS

*T*he Christmas story began in the little town of Bethlehem, in a manger. It was there, in the most humble of circumstances, that God fulfilled His Old Testament promise by offering salvation to the world. Not far from that manger, shepherds were tending their flock:

> And it came to pass in those days that a decree went out from Caesar Augustus that all the world should be registered. This census first took place while Quirinius was governing Syria. So all went to be registered, everyone to his own city. Joseph also went up from Galilee, out of the city of Nazareth, into Judea, to the city of David, which is called Bethlehem, because he was of the house and

lineage of David, to be registered with Mary, his betrothed wife, who was with child. So it was, that while they were there, the days were completed for her to be delivered. And she brought forth her first-born Son, and wrapped Him in swaddling cloths, and laid Him in a manger, because there was no room for them in the inn. Now there were in the same country shepherds living out in the fields, keeping watch over their flock by night. And behold, an angel of the Lord stood before them, and the glory of the Lord shone around them, and they were greatly afraid. Then the angel said to them, "Do not be afraid, for behold, I bring you good tidings of great joy which will be to all people. For there is born to you this day in the city of David a Savior, who is Christ the Lord. And this will be the sign to you: You will find a Babe wrapped in swaddling cloths, lying in a manger." And suddenly there was with the angel a multitude of the heavenly host praising God and saying: "Glory to God in the highest, And on earth peace, goodwill toward men!" (Luke 2:1-14 NKJV)

These familiar words from the second chapter of Luke remind us that the Lord's greatest gift was presented to mankind in the form of a babe, wrapped in simple swaddling clothes, laid in a manger.

The Christ child changed the world forever, and He can do the same for us. On this Christmas day, we, like the shepherds of old, are called to celebrate the birth of the baby named Jesus. May we, like those shepherds, leave our fields—wherever they may be—and pause to worship God's priceless Christmas gift: His Son.

Jesus Christ was born into this world,
not from it.

Oswald Chambers

The whole meaning of Christmas
can be summed up in the miracle
of Christ's birth.

Arthur Bryant

*All the earth shall worship You and sing praises*
*to You; they shall sing praises to Your name.*

Psalm 66:4 NKJV

All praise to Thee, Eternal Lord,
clothed in a garb of flesh and blood,
choosing a manger for a throne.

Martin Luther

The manger is a symbol of what can happen
when Jesus Christ resides inside us.
The ordinary suddenly becomes
extraordinary.

Bill Hybels

The magic message of Christmas is that
God gave us so much more than
we can possibly give back!

Norman Vincent Peale

Jesus Christ founded His Kingdom
on the weakest link of all: a Baby.

Oswald Chambers

The old message "For unto you is born
this day in the city of David a Savior
which is Christ the Lord"
is still the heart of Christmas.

Peter Marshall

*For the Son of Man has come to save the lost.*

Matthew 18:11 HCSB

Infinite, and an infant.
Eternal, and yet born of a woman.
Heir of all things, yet the carpenter's son.

C. H. Spurgeon

The Son of God became man to enable men
to become sons of God.

C. S. Lewis

*For God did not send His Son into the world*
*that He might judge the world,*
*but that the world might be saved through Him.*

John 3:17 HCSB

Even before God created the heavens
and the earth, He knew you and me,
and He chose us! You and I were born
because it was God's good pleasure.

Kay Arthur

The grace of God is infinite and eternal.
As it had no beginning, so it can have
no end, and being an attribute of God,
it is as boundless as infinitude.

A. W. Tozer

If you have a true faith that Christ is your
Savior, then at once you have a gracious God,
for faith leads you in and opens up God's heart
and will, that you should see pure grace
and overflowing love.

Martin Luther

*For I am persuaded that neither death nor life, nor angels nor rulers, nor things present, nor things to come, nor powers, nor height, nor depth, nor any other created thing will have the power to separate us from the love of God that is in Christ Jesus our Lord!*

—

Romans 8:38-39 HCSB

---

Go tell it on the mountain,
over the hills and everywhere.
Go tell it on the mountain,
that Jesus Christ is born!

—

Traditional American Spiritual

---

# CHAPTER 2

# THE JOY OF CHRISTMAS

*T*he Christmas season is a time for joy and celebration. In the hamlet of Bethlehem, God gave the world a priceless gift: the Christ child. We, as believers, can rejoice: God, through His Son, has offered spiritual abundance and salvation to the world.

During our earthly existence, of course, we will all have trials and troubles—but as believers we are secure. God has promised us peace, joy, and eternal life. So, as we join in the celebrations of this sacred holiday, let us rejoice in God's most glorious gift: a baby born in a manger, a baby who forever changed the world. And then, with hope in our hearts and praise on our lips, let the celebration begin!

Rejoice, that the immortal God is born,
so that mortal man may live in eternity.

Jan Hus

Christ and joy go together.

E. Stanley Jones

Joyful, joyful, we adore thee,
God of glory, Lord of love.
Hearts unfold like flowers before thee;
opening to the sun above.

Henry Van Dyke

Where the soul is full of peace and joy,
outward surroundings and circumstances are
of comparatively little account.

Hannah Whitall Smiith

True happiness and contentment cannot
come from the things of this world.
The blessedness of true joy is a free gift
that comes only from our Lord and Savior,
Jesus Christ.

Dennis Swanberg

*Rejoice always, pray without ceasing,
in everything give thanks; for this is the will of
God in Christ Jesus for you.*

1 Thessalonians 5:16-18 NKJV

God can take any man and
put the miracle of His joy into him.

Oswald Chambers

When we bring sunshine into the lives of
others, we're warmed by it ourselves. When
we spill a little happiness, it splashes on us.

Barbara Johnson

Our God is so wonderfully good, and lovely,
and blessed in every way that the mere fact
of belonging to Him is enough for
an untellable fullness of joy!

Hannah Whitall Smith

Joy comes not from what we have
but from what we are.

C. H. Spurgeon

Happiness is the by-product of a life that
is lived in the will of God.
When we humbly serve others,
walk in God's path of holiness,
and do what He tells us,
then we will enjoy happiness.

Warren Wiersbe

*Rejoice in the Lord, you righteous ones;*
*praise from the upright is beautiful.*

Psalm 33:1 HCSB

Joy is the direct result of having
God's perspective on our daily lives and
the effect of loving our Lord enough to obey
His commands and trust His promises.

Bill Bright

Joy cannot be pursued. It comes from
within. It is a state of being. It does not
depend on circumstances, but triumphs over
circumstances. It produces a gentleness of
spirit and a magnetic personality.

Billy Graham

*Rejoice in the Lord always.*
*I will say it again: Rejoice!*

Philippians 4:4 HCSB

When I think of Christmas Eves,
Christmas feasts, Christmas songs,
and Christmas stories,
I know it was not a short
and transient gladness.
It was—and is—a joy unspeakable
and full of glory.

—

Corrie ten Boom

*This is the day the LORD
has made; we will rejoice
and be glad in it.*

—

Psalm 118:24 NKJV

# CHAPTER 3

# THE PROMISE OF CHRISTMAS

*I have spoken these things to you
so that My joy may be in you
and your joy may be complete.*

John 15:11 HCSB

The prophecies of the Old Testament foretell the promise of Christmas: "For a child will be born for us, a son will be given to us, and the government will be on His shoulders. He will be named Wonderful Counselor, Mighty God, Eternal Father, Prince of Peace" (Isaiah 9:6 HCSB). In Bethlehem, God fulfilled His promise on that joyful night when a babe was born in a manger. And every year at Christmastime, we celebrate the birth of the Christ child, God's priceless gift to the world.

Christ made it clear: He intends that His joy should become our joy. Yet sometimes, amid the inevitable hustle and bustle of life, we can forfeit—albeit temporarily—the joy of Christ as we wrestle with the challenges of daily living.

Jonathan Edwards, the 18th-century American clergyman, observed, "Christ is not only a remedy for your weariness and trouble, but he will give you an abundance of the contrary: joy and delight. They who come to Christ do not only come to a resting-place after they have been wandering in a wilderness, but they come to a banqueting-house where they may rest, and where they may feast. They may cease from their former troubles and toils, and they may enter upon a course of delights and spiritual joys."

This year's Christmas celebration provides yet another opportunity to praise God for His infinite love and for His incalculable gifts. May you and yours celebrate both.

Jesus came into the world so we could know,
once and for all, that God is concerned
about the way we live, the way we believe,
and the way we die.

Billy Graham

The Son of God does not want to be seen
and found in heaven. Therefore he descended
from heaven to this earth and came
to us in our flesh.

Martin Luther

Jesus is the personal approach from
the unseen God coming so near that he
becomes inescapable. You don't have to
find him—you just have to consent
to be found.

E. Stanley Jones

What a paradox that a babe
in a manger should be called
mighty! Yet even as a babe,
Jesus Christ was the center of
power. His birth affected
the heavens and caused
a dazzling star to appear.
Midnight became midday
as the glory of the Lord
appeared to men.

—

Warren Wiersbe

Christmas means the beginning of
Christianity—and a second chance
for the world.

Peter Marshall

If we could condense all the truths of
Christmas into only three words,
these would be the words: "God with us."

John MacArthur

The miracle of Christmas is not
on 34th Street; it's in Bethlehem.

Rick Warren

The Word had become flesh,
a real human baby. He had not ceased to be
God. He was no less God then than before,
but He had begun to be man. He was not now
God minus some elements of His deity but
God plus all that He had made His own by
taking manhood to himself.

J. I. Packer

The crucial question for each of us is this:
What do you think of Jesus, and do you yet
have a personal acquaintance with Him?

Hannah Whitall Smith

Tell me the story of Jesus.
Write on my heart every word.
Tell me the story most precious,
sweetest that ever was heard.

—

Fanny Crosby

Just as Our Lord came into human history
from outside, so He must come into me
from outside. Have I allowed my personal
human life to become a "Bethlehem"
for the Son of God?

Oswald Chambers

On Christmas Day two thousand years ago,
the birth of a tiny baby in an obscure village
in the Middle East was God's supreme
triumph of good over evil.

Charles Colson

Jesus—the standard of measurement,
the scale of weights, the test of character for
the whole moral universe.

R. G. Lee

So Jesus came, stripping himself of everything
as he came—omnipotence, omniscience,
omnipresence—everything except love.
"He emptied himself" (Philippians 2:7),
emptied himself of everything except love.
Love—his only protection, his only weapon,
his only method.

E. Stanley Jones

He loved us not because we're lovable,
but because He is love.

C. S. Lewis

Being a Christian is more than just
an instantaneous conversion; it is like
a daily process whereby you grow to be
more and more like Christ.

Billy Graham

Then let every heart keep
Christmas within.
Christ's pity for sorrow,
Christ's hatred for sin,
Christ's care for the weakest,
Christ's courage for right,
Everywhere, everywhere,
Christmas tonight!

—

Phillips Brooks

*My lips will shout for joy when*
*I sing praise to You.*

Psalm 71:23 HCSB

*Shout to the Lord, all the earth; be jubilant,*
*shout for joy, and sing.*

Psalm 98:4 HCSB

*I will thank the Lord with all my heart;*
*I will declare all Your wonderful works.*
*I will rejoice and boast about You;*
*I will sing about Your name, Most High.*

Psalm 9:1-2 HCSB

Claim the joy that is yours.
Pray.
And know that your joy
is used by God to reach others.

—

Kay Arthur

# CHAPTER 4

# CHRISTMAS IS . . .

*C*hristmas is the glorious day on which we celebrate that pivotal event in human history, the birth of Christ. No amount of commercialism or fanfare should obscure the fact that Christmastime is the annual birthday celebration for the Christian faith, a time for believers everywhere to rejoice, to pray, and to give thanks for God's greatest treasure: His Son.

Billy Graham observed, "Christmas is the celebration of the event that set Heaven to singing, an event that gave the stars of the night sky a new brilliance." As we prepare for the busy days that lead up to Christmas, it is appropriate that we remain mindful of the real reason for the holiday season by offering our prayers and our praise to the One whose birth we celebrate.

Christmas is about a baby,
born in a stable,
who changed the world forever.

—

John Maxwell

Christmas is the day that holds
all time together.

—

Alexander Smith

Christmas, like God,
is timeless and eternal.

Dale Evans

Christmas is not just a day of the year.
It is also—and more importantly—
a condition of the heart.

Marie T. Freeman

The Christmas message
is that there is hope for
humanity, hope of pardon,
hope of peace with God,
hope of glory.

—

J. I. Packer

The Christmas story gives its triumphant
answer: "Be not afraid."

Karl Barth

The Christmas spirit—love—
changes hearts and lives.

Pat Boone

If Christmas is about anything, Christmas is
the story of God changing worlds and putting
limitations upon Himself. It's the story
of a baby born in Bethlehem, who was much
more powerful than the Roman Empire
that existed that day.

John Maxwell

Christmas, my child,
is love in action.
Every time we love,
every time we give,
it's Christmas.

—

Dale Evans

*Then Jesus spoke to them again:
"I am the light of the world.
Anyone who follows Me will
never walk in the darkness,
but will have the light of life."*

—

John 8:12 HCSB

# CHAPTER 5

# SHARING CHRIST'S GIFTS

The old familiar hymn begins, "What a friend we have in Jesus . . . ." No truer words were ever penned. Christ showed enduring love by willingly sacrificing His own life so that we might have eternal life. As believers, we are blessed beyond measure—and God calls upon us to share our blessings.

Christmas is the season for giving, but gift-giving need not be synonymous with commercialism. The holiday season is the perfect time to share spiritual gifts as well as material ones. Spiritual gifts, of course, should take priority, but we must also give freely of our possessions, especially to those in need.

The words of Jesus are unambiguous: "Freely you have received, freely give" (Matthew

10:8 NKJV). May this holiday season, and every one hereafter, be a time when we, as followers of Christ, show our love for Him through the generosity that we show to others.

To celebrate the heart
of Christmas is to
forget ourselves in
the service of others.

—

Henry C. Link

This is Christmas, the real meaning of it:
God loving, searching, giving Himself to us;
man needing, receiving, giving himself to
God. Redemption's glorious exchange of gifts,
without which we cannot live, without which
we cannot give to those we love anything
of lasting value. This is the meaning of
Christmas, the wonder and the glory of it.

Ruth Bell Graham

*The righteous give and don't hold back.*

Proverbs 21:26 HCSB

Let us give according to our incomes,
lest God make our incomes match our gifts.

Peter Marshall

Let us remember that the Christmas heart is a giving heart, a wide-open heart that thinks of others first. The birth of the baby Jesus stands as the most significant event in all history because it has meant the pouring into a sick world of the healing medicine of love which has transformed all manner of hearts for almost two thousand years.

George Matthew Adams

*Whatever you did for one of the least of these brothers of Mine, you did for Me.*

Matthew 25:40 HCSB

*So let each one give as he
purposes in his heart,
not grudgingly or of necessity;
for God loves a cheerful giver.*

—

2 Corinthians 9:7 NKJV

Abundant living means abundant giving.

E. Stanley Jones

A happy spirit takes the grind out of giving.
The grease of gusto frees
the gears of generosity.

Charles Swindoll

Generosity is changing one's focus
from self to others.

John Maxwell

It is the duty of every Christian to be
Christ to his neighbor.

Martin Luther

The measure of a life, after all,
is not its duration but its donation.

Corrie ten Boom

Selfishness is as far from Christianity
as darkness is from light.

C. H. Spurgeon

Giving to God and, in His name,
to others, is not something that we do;
it the result of what we are.

Warren Wiersbe

*And may the Lord make you increase*
*and abound in love to one another and to all.*

1 Thessalonians 3:12 NKJV

Jesus had a loving heart.
If he dwells within us,
hatred and bitterness
will never rule us.

—

Billy Graham

Christmas is most truly
Christmas when we celebrate it
by giving the light of love
to those who need it most.

—

Ruth Carter Stapleton

# CHAPTER 6

# WORSHIPPING THE CHRIST CHILD

*N*othing should obscure the fact that Christmastime is the annual birthday celebration of the Christian faith. Christmas day is, above all else, a religious holiday—a time for Christians everywhere to rejoice, to pray, and to worship God.

The 25th day of December, like every other day of the year, provides countless opportunities to put God where He belongs: at the center of our lives. When we do so, we are blessed.

During this holiday season, it is proper that we keep our eyes, our voices, and our hearts lifted upward as we offer profound thanksgiving to God through our worship and our praise.

On Christmas, we celebrate the day when
the Son of God became the Son of Man.
We celebrate the day when the Son of
the Highest stooped to the lowest,
a day when the King of Glory shed his
splendor and became poor that we,
through his poverty, might be rich.

Arthur M. Brazier

Worship is wonder, love, and praise.
Not only does it cause us to contemplate
and appreciate our holy God, but it gives us
vitality, vigor, and a desire to obey Him.

Franklin Graham

In commanding us to glorify Him,
God is inviting us to enjoy Him.

C. S. Lewis

In the sanctuary, we discover beauty:
the beauty of His presence.

Kay Arthur

*I rejoiced with those who said to me,*
*"Let us go to the house of the Lord."*

Psalm 122:1 HCSB

Praise and thank God for who He is
and for what He has done for you.

Billy Graham

The fact that we were created to enjoy God
and to worship him forever
is etched upon our souls.

Jim Cymbala

Praise Him! Praise Him!
Tell of His excellent greatness.
Praise Him! Praise Him!
Ever in joyful song!

Fanny Crosby

*Praise the Lord!*
*Oh, give thanks to the Lord, for He is good!*
*For His mercy endures forever.*

Psalm 106:1 NKJV

*But an hour is coming, and is now here,
when the true worshipers will worship the Father
in spirit and truth. Yes, the Father wants such
people to worship Him. God is Spirit,
and those who worship Him must worship
in spirit and truth.*

John 4:23-24 HCSB

*I am the bread of life, Jesus told them.
"No one who comes to Me will ever be hungry,
and no one who believes in Me
will ever be thirsty again."*

John 6:35 HCSB

There's no better time than Christmas to
become the kind of seeker the wise men
embodied. Wise people still seek Christ.

Rick Warren

*He is the image of the invisible God, the firstborn
over all creation; because by Him everything was
created, in heaven and on earth, the visible and
the invisible, whether thrones or dominions or
rulers or authorities—all things have been
created through Him and for Him.*

Colossians 1:15-16 HCSB

*For where two or three are gathered together
in My name, I am there among them.*

Matthew 18:20 HCSB

It is impossible to worship God
and remain unchanged.

Henry Blackaby

Worship is not taught from the pulpit.
It must be learned in the heart.

Jim Elliot

Worship is a voluntary act of gratitude
offered by the saved to the Savior,
by the healed to the Healer,
by the delivered to the Deliverer.

Max Lucado

*Therefore, through Him let us continually
offer up to God a sacrifice of praise, that is,
the fruit of our lips that confess His name.*

Hebrews 13:15 HCSB

Worship is your spirit responding to
God's Spirit.

Rick Warren

Worship and worry cannot live
in the same heart;
they are mutually exclusive.

Ruth Bell Graham

It's our privilege to not only raise our hands
in worship but also to combine the visible
with the invisible in a rising stream of praise
and adoration sent directly to our Father.

Shirley Dobson

Spiritual worship comes from our very core
and is fueled by an awesome reverence
and desire for God.

Beth Moore

Nothing we do is more powerful or
more life-changing than praising God.

Stormie Omartian

Our God is the sovereign Creator of
the universe! He loves us as His own children
and has provided every good thing we have;
He is worthy of our praise every moment.

Shirley Dobson

It's the definition of worship:
A hungry heart finding the Father's feast.
A searching soul finding the Father's face.
A wandering pilgrim spotting the Father's
house. Finding God. Finding God seeking us.
This is worship. This is a worshiper.

Max Lucado

Worship is wonder, love, and praise.
Not only does it cause us to contemplate
and appreciate our holy God, but it gives us
vitality, vigor, and a desire to obey Him.

Franklin Graham

In commanding us to glorify Him,
God is inviting us to enjoy Him.

C. S. Lewis

———

The time for universal praise is
sure to come some day.
Let us begin to do our part now.

—

Hannah Whitall Smith

———

# CHAPTER 7

# JOYFUL SONGS OF CELEBRATION AND PRAISE

*A*s we grow older many things about Christmas change. But some things remain the same, including the songs that we sing. When it comes to Yuletide fare, our musical tastes are slow to change. Thank goodness.

The songs of Christmas, especially our favorite hymns, rank among the most beloved compositions ever penned. On the pages that follow, we celebrate a few of the songs we sing at Christmastime: May these holiday classics remain unchanged forever.

# AWAY IN A MANGER

Away in a manger,
no crib for a bed,
The little Lord Jesus
lay down his sweet head.
The stars in the sky
looked down where he lay,
The little Lord Jesus,
asleep on the hay.

The cattle are lowing,
the baby awakes,
But little Lord Jesus,
no crying he makes.
I love Thee, Lord Jesus!
Look down from the sky,
And stay by my cradle
till morning is nigh.

Be near me, Lord Jesus,
I ask Thee to stay
Close by me forever,
and love me, I pray.
Bless all the dear children
in thy tender care,
And take us to heaven,
to live with Thee there.

—

Anonymous

# GOD REST YOU
# MERRY GENTLEMEN

God rest you merry, gentlemen,
Let nothing you dismay,
Remember Christ our Savior
Was born on Christmas Day,
To save us all from Satan's pow'r
When we were gone astray;
O tidings of comfort and joy,
comfort and joy,
O tidings of comfort and joy.

From God our heavenly Father,
A blessed angel came.
And unto certain shepherds,
Brought tidings of the same;
How that in Bethlehem was born
The Son of God by name;
O tidings of comfort and joy,
comfort and joy,
O tidings of comfort and joy.

—

Traditional 17th-Century English Carol

# IT CAME UPON THE MIDNIGHT CLEAR

It came upon the midnight clear,
that glorious song of old,
From angels bending near the earth,
to touch their harps of gold.
Peace on the earth, goodwill to men,
from heav'n's all gracious king,
The world in solemn stillness lay
to hear the angels sing.

For lo! the days are hastening on,
By prophets seen of old,
When with the ever-circling years
Shall come the time foretold,
When peace shall over all the earth
Its ancient splendors fling,
And the whole world give back the song
Which now the angels sing.

—

Edmund Sears, 1850

# SILENT NIGHT

Silent Night! Holy Night!
All is calm, all is bright.
Round yon virgin mother and child!
Holy infant so tender and mild,
Sleep in heavenly peace,
sleep in heavenly peace.

Silent Night! Holy Night!
Shepherds quake at the sight!
Glories stream from heaven afar,
Heavenly hosts sing Alleluia!
Christ the Savior is born!
Christ the Savior is born!

Silent Night! Holy Night!
Son of God, love's pure light;
Radiant beams from Thy holy face,
with the dawn of redeeming grace,
Jesus Lord, at Thy birth,
Jesus Lord, at Thy birth.

—

Father Joseph Mohr, 1818

# JOY TO THE WORLD

Joy to the world! the Lord is come:
Let earth receive her King;
Let every heart prepare him room,
And heaven and nature sing.
And heaven and nature sing.
And heaven, and heaven, and nature sing.

Joy to the world! the Saviour reigns:
Let men their songs employ;
While fields and floods, rocks, hills, and plains
Repeat the sounding joy.
Repeat the sounding joy.
Repeat, repeat the sounding joy.

He rules the world with truth and grace,
And makes the nations prove
The glories of his righteousness,
And wonders of his love.
And wonders of his love.
And wonders, wonders of his love.

—

Words by Isaac Watts (1674-1748)
Music by Lowell Mason (1792-1872)

# THE FIRST NOEL

The first Noel the angel did say
Was to certain poor shepherds
in fields as they lay;
In fields as they lay, keeping their sheep,
On a cold winter's night that was so deep.

Noel, Noel, Noel, Noel,
Born is the King of Israel.

They looked up and saw a star
Shining in the east beyond them far,
And to the earth it gave great light,
And so it continued both day and night.

Noel, Noel, Noel, Noel,
Born is the King of Israel.

Then entered in those wise men three
Full reverently upon their knee,
and offered there in his presence
Their gold, and myrrh, and frankincense.

Noel, Noel, Noel, Noel,
Born is the King of Israel.

Then let us all with one accord
Sing praises to our heavenly Lord;
That hath made heaven and earth of naught,
And with his blood mankind hath bought.

—

Traditional English Carol

# O LITTLE TOWN OF BETHLEHEM

O little town of Bethlehem,
How still we see thee lie,
Above thy deep and dreamless sleep,
The silent stars go by;
Yet in thy dark streets shineth
The everlasting Light,
The hopes and fears of all the years
Are met in thee tonight.

For Christ is born of Mary,
And gathered all above,
While mortals sleep, the angels keep
Their watch of wondering love.
O morning stars, together
Proclaim the holy birth!
And praises sing to God the King,
And peace to men on earth.

How silently, how silently,
The wondrous gift is giv'n!
So God imparts to human hearts
The blessings of His heav'n.
No ear may hear His coming,
But in this world of sin,
Where meek souls will receive Him, still
The dear Christ enters in.

O holy Child of Bethlehem!
Descend to us we pray;
Cast out our sin and enter in,
Be born in us today.
We hear the Christmas angels
The great glad tidings tell;
O come to us abide with us,
Our Lord Emmanuel!

—

Phillips Brooks, 1868

# HARK! THE HERALD ANGELS SING

Hark! the herald angels sing,
"Glory to the newborn King.
Peace on earth and mercy mild;
God and sinners reconciled."
Joyful all ye nations rise.
Join the triumph of the skies;
with angelic host proclaim,
"Christ is born in Bethlehem!"
Hark! The herald angels sing,
"Glory to the newborn King."

Charles Wesley, 1739

# CHAPTER 8

# A TIME FOR FAMILY AND FRIENDS

*C*hristmas is a time for going home. And even when we can't enjoy the physical presence of family and friends, we can still find a special place for them in our hearts.

Christmas is a season when families gather to share food, songs, stories, and memories. Holiday celebrations bring us together, and holiday traditions remind us of our heritage.

This holiday season, like every other, should be a time of thanksgiving and fellowship. And, amid the holiday happenings, let us always remember the One who came to earth so that we might have abundance and salvation. Jesus said, "As the Father loved Me, I also have loved you; abide in My love" (John 15:9 NKJV). He first loved us; let us return His love by sharing it.

A Christmas family-party! We know of nothing in nature more delightful!

—

Charles Dickens

*Unless the Lord builds a house, its builders labor
over it in vain; unless the Lord watches over
a city, the watchman stays alert in vain.*

Psalm 127:1 HCSB

*A new commandment I give to you,
that you love one another; as I have loved you,
that you also love one another.*

John 13:34 NKJV

*Now these three remain: faith, hope, and love.
But the greatest of these is love.*

1 Corinthians 13:13 HCSB

Christmas is about family:
God's family . . . and yours.

Jim Gallery

A family is a place where principles
are hammered and honed on the anvil
of everyday living.

Charles Swindoll

Our homes and families can sometimes be
sources of struggle. But His reality is,
for every family, a source of constant care.
Doesn't that feel good at Christmas?

Calvin Miller

Apart from religious influence,
the family is the most important
influence on society.

Billy Graham

The God who adopted you into
His forever family knows how to make
earthly families work.

Charles Stanley

When the family is together on Christmas
day, all is well with the world!

Marie T. Freeman

*Choose for yourselves today
the one you will worship . . . .
As for me and my family,
we will worship the Lord.*

—

Joshua 24:15 HCSB

# CHAPTER 9

## JOYFUL CHRISTMAS MEMORIES

*C*hristmas is a time for memories: revisiting old ones and making new ones. If we're lucky and wise, we do both.

No season carries with it as many reminiscences as the holiday season. As December 25th approaches, we are confronted with a double dose of memory-evoking events: the end of another year and the passing of another Christmas. No wonder we find ourselves reflecting on the past.

This year, as we celebrate this holiday season and give thanks for the ones that have gone before, let us thank God for all His blessings: past, present, and future. And let us keep our happy memories of Christmases past forever in our hearts.

Christmas: that magic blanket that wraps
itself about us, that something so intangible
that it is like a fragrance. It may weave
a spell of nostalgia. Christmas may be a day of
feasting, or of prayer, but always it will be
a day of remembrance, a day in which
we think of everything we have ever loved.

Augusta E. Rundel

Happy, happy Christmas, that can win us back
to the delusions of our childhood days, recall
to the old man the pleasures of his youth,
and transport the traveler back to his own
fireside and quiet home!

Charles Dickens

Christmas is a good time to take stock
of our blessings.

Pat Boone

As another Christmas passes, the memory
of it stays and hovers like the scent of cedar.
And even if it can't be Christmas all the year,
memories remain.

Minnie Pearl

Line by line, moment by moment, special
times are etched into our memories in
the permanent ink of everlasting love
in our relationships.

Gloria Gaither

During the Christmas season,
I hope that your own times
of excitement and sharing
and fellowship will leave you
with a special gift—memories
that will last a lifetime.

—

James Dobson

# CHAPTER 10

# A SEASON OF PRAYER

The Christmas season is a time when we offer thanks for Jesus and for the One who sent Him. We express thanksgiving through our words, through our deeds, and through our prayers.

Jesus instructed His followers to pray always, and His advice applies to Christians of every generation. When we weave the habit of prayer into the very fabric of our days, we invite God to become a partner in every aspect of our lives. And, when we make the Christmas season a time of thanksgiving and prayer, we welcome the Christ child into our hearts, which, of course, is exactly where He belongs.

A life growing in its purity and devotion
will be a more prayerful life.

E. M. Bounds

Obedience is the master key
to effective prayer.

Billy Graham

Prayer guards hearts and minds
and causes God to bring peace
out of chaos.

Beth Moore

Two wings are necessary to lift our souls
toward God: prayer and praise.
Prayer asks.
Praise accepts the answer.

Mrs. Charles E. Cowman

Find a place to pray where no one imagines
that you are praying.
Then, shut the door and talk to God.

Oswald Chambers

Prayer connects us with
God's limitless potential.

Henry Blackaby

*And everything—whatever you ask in prayer,*
*believing—you will receive.*
Matthew 21:22 HCSB

*Keep asking, and it will be given to you.*
*Keep searching, and you will find.*
*Keep knocking, and the door will be opened to*
*you. For everyone who asks receives,*
*and the one who searches finds, and to the one*
*who knocks, the door will be opened.*
Matthew 7:7-8 HCSB

*The intense prayer of the righteous*
*is very powerful.*
James 5:16 HCSB

God makes prayer as easy as possible for us.
He's completely approachable and available,
and He'll never mock or upbraid us for
bringing our needs before Him.

Shirley Dobson

When will we realize that we're not troubling
God with our questions and concerns?
His heart is open to hear us—his touch nearer
than our next thought—as if no one in the
world existed but us. Our very personal God
wants to hear from us personally.

Gigi Graham Tchividjian

God will help us become the people we are
meant to be, if only we will ask Him.

Hannah Whitall Smith

———

*Rejoice always! Pray constantly.*
*Give thanks in everything,*
*for this is God's will for you*
*in Christ Jesus.*

—

1 Thessalonians 5:16-18 HCSB

# CHAPTER 11

# THE TIME FOR RENEWAL

rom time to time, we may find ourselves running on empty, especially at Christmastime. The pressing demands of the holiday season may temporarily rob us of the joy and the peace that might otherwise be ours through Christ.

When the obligations of Christmas drain our strength and test our patience, there is a source from which we can draw the power and the perspective needed to recharge our spiritual batteries. That source is God.

If we genuinely lift our hearts and prayers to our Heavenly Father, He renews our strength. And, when we take time to study God's Word, we are confronted with a profound truth: the challenges of today will soon fade away, but God's love endures forever.

I'm ever and always a stranger to grace.
I need this annual angel visitation to know
the virgin conceives and God is with us.

Eugene Peterson

No matter how badly we have failed,
we can always get up and begin again.
Our God is the God of new beginnings.

Warren Wiersbe

*Create in me a clean heart, O God,*
*and renew a steadfast spirit within me.*

Psalm 51:10 NKJV

He is the God of wholeness and restoration.

Stormie Om'artian

God specializes in things fresh and firsthand.
His plans for you this year may outshine those
of the past. He's prepared to fill your days
with reasons to give Him praise.

Joni Eareckson Tada

Whoever you are, whatever your condition or
circumstance, whatever your past or problem,
Jesus can restore you to wholeness.

Anne Graham Lotz

When we invite Jesus
into our lives,
we experience life in the fullest,
most vital sense.

—

Catherine Marshall

God is the One who provides our strength,
not only to cope with the demands
of the day, but also to rise above them.
May we look to Him for the strength to soar.

Jim Gallery

When we spend time with Christ,
He supplies us with strength and encourages
us in the pursuit of His ways.

Elizabeth George

A divine strength is given to those who yield
themselves to the Father and obey what
He tells them to do.

Warren Wiersbe

*But those who wait on the Lord*
*Shall renew their strength;*
*They shall mount up with wings like eagles,*
*They shall run and not be weary,*
*They shall walk and not faint.*

Isaiah 40:31 NKJV

Father, for this day, renew within me
the gift of the Holy Spirit.

Andrew Murray

*Then He who sat on the throne said,*
*"Behold, I make all things new."*

Revelation 21:5 NKJV

God is great and God is powerful,
but we must invite him to be powerful
in our lives. His strength is always there,
but it's up to us to provide a channel through
which that power can flow.

Bill Hybels

The amazing thing about Jesus is that
He doesn't just patch up our lives,
He gives us a brand new sheet,
a clean slate to start over, all new.

Gloria Gaither

*Therefore if anyone is in Christ,
he is a new creature;
the old things passed away;
behold, new things have come.*

—

2 Corinthians 5:17 HCSB

# CHAPTER 12

# CELEBRATING GOD'S PROMISES

*T*he words of Matthew 4:4 remind us that, "Man shall not live by bread alone, but by every word that proceeds from the mouth of God" (NKJV). During the season when we celebrate the birth of God's Son, we should study the Bible and meditate upon its meaning for our lives. Otherwise, we deprive ourselves of a priceless gift from our Creator.

God has given us the Holy Bible for the purpose of knowing His promises, His power, His commandments, His wisdom, His love, and His Son. As we study God's teachings and apply them to our lives, we live by the Word that shall never pass away.

God did not write a book and send it by
messenger to be read at a distance by unaided
minds. He spoke a Book and lives in
His spoken words, constantly speaking
His words and causing the power of them
to persist across the years.

A. W. Tozer

The most important thing about the Bible is
that it points us to the living Word of God,
which is Jesus Christ.

Billy Graham

How do you wait upon the Lord?
First you must learn to sit at His feet
and take time to listen to His words.

Kay Arthur

*Heaven and earth will pass away,*
*but My words will never pass away.*

Matthew 24:35 HCSB

*All Scripture is inspired by God and is profitable*
*for teaching, for rebuking, for correcting,*
*for training in righteousness, so that the man*
*of God may be complete,*
*equipped for every good work.*

2 Timothy 3:16-17 HCSB

*Your word is a lamp to my feet*
*and a light to my path.*

Psalm 119:105 NKJV

Nobody ever outgrows Scripture;
the book widens and deepens with our years.

C. H. Spurgeon

The Gospel is not so much a demand
as it is an offer, an offer of new life
to man by the grace of God.

E. Stanley Jones

The only way we can understand
the Bible is by personal contact
with the Living Word.

Oswald Chambers

The Holy Scriptures are
our letters from home.

—

St. Augustine

Weave the unveiling fabric of God's Word
through your heart and mind. It will hold
strong, even if the rest of life unravels.

Gigi Graham Tchividjian

God can see clearly no matter how dark
or foggy the night is.
Trust His Word to guide you safely home.

Lisa Whelchel

As we spend time reading, applying, and
obeying our Bibles, the Spirit of Truth
Who is also the Spirit of Jesus increasingly
reveals Jesus to us.

Anne Graham Lotz

The Scriptures were not given
for our information,
but for our transformation.

D. L. Moody

When the child of God looks into
the Word of God, he sees the Son of God.
And, he is transformed by the Spirit
of God to share in the glory of God.

Warren Wiersbe

The Bible is the cradle wherein
Christ is laid.

Martin Luther

Words fail to express my love for this
holy Book, my gratitude for its author,
for His love and goodness.
How shall I thank him for it?

Lottie Moon

If you want to know God as he speaks to you
through the Bible, you should study
the Bible daily, systematically,
comprehensively, devotionally,
and prayerfully.

James Montgomery Boice

The stars may fall,
but God's promises will stand
and be fulfilled.

—

J. I. Packer

The vigor of our spiritual lives
will be in exact proportion
to the place held by
the Bible in our lives
and in our thoughts.

—

George Mueller

# CHAPTER 13

# SHARING THE JOY AND GOOD CHEER

*C*hristmas is the perfect time to share feelings of joy and good cheer. And, of course, the more good feelings we share, the more we have left over for ourselves.

The Christian life is a cause for celebration. Christ promises us a life of abundance, wholeness, and joy, but He does not force His joy upon us. We must claim His promises for ourselves, and when we do, Jesus, in turn, fills our spirits with His power and His love. Then, as God's children, we can share Christ's joy and His message with a world that needs both.

Christ can put a spring in your step
and a thrill in your heart.
Optimism and cheerfulness are products
of knowing Christ.

Billy Graham

Christmas began in the heart of God.
It is complete only when it reaches
the heart of man.

Anonymous

When we bring sunshine into the lives of
others, we're warmed by it ourselves.
When we spill a little happiness,
it splashes on us.

Barbara Johnson

Make the least of all that goes and the most
of all that comes. Don't regret what is past.
Cherish what you have.
Look forward to all that is to come.
And most important of all,
rely moment by moment on Jesus Christ.

Gigi Graham Tchividjian

Perhaps the best Yuletide decoration
is being wreathed in smiles.

Anonymous

*The Lord reigns; let the earth rejoice.*

Psalm 97:1 NKJV

A smile is the light in the window of your face
that tells people you're at home.

Barbara Johnson

Life goes on.
Keep on smiling and the whole world
smiles with you.

Dennis Swanberg

*A cheerful heart
has a continual feast.*

—

Proverbs 15:15 HCSB

If you can keep
Christmas for a day,
why not always?

—

Henry van Dyke

# CHAPTER 14

# STRENGTH FOR THE HOLIDAYS

As December 25th grows closer, we may find ourselves feeling exhausted or worse. The unrelenting demands of the holiday season may temporarily rob us of the joy and the peace that might otherwise be ours through Christ.

When the inevitable pressures of the holiday season sap our strength or test our patience, there is a source from which we can draw the power we need to recharge our spiritual batteries. That source is God.

If we genuinely lift our hearts and prayers to our Heavenly Father, He renews our strength. Our task, of course, is to let Him.

The same God who empowered Samson,
Gideon, and Paul seeks to empower my life
and your life, because God hasn't changed.

Bill Hybels

~

Just as omitting an essential vitamin from
our diet will make us physically weak,
so a lack of prayer will make us
spiritually anemic.

Billy Graham

~

If we take God's program,
we can have God's power—not otherwise.

E. Stanley Jones

*Finally, be strengthened by the Lord
and by His vast strength.*

Ephesians 6:10 HCSB

~

*You, therefore, my child, be strong
in the grace that is in Christ Jesus.*

2 Timothy 2:1 HCSB

~

*The Lord is my strength and my song;
He has become my salvation.*

Exodus 15:2 HCSB

All the power of God—the same power
that hung the stars in place and put
the planets in their courses and transformed
Earth—now resides in you to energize
and strengthen you to become the person
God created you to be.

Anne Graham Lotz

No matter how heavy the burden,
daily strength is given, so I expect we need
not give ourselves any concern as to what
the outcome will be.
We must simply go forward.

Annie Armstrong

God's help is always available,
but it is only given to those who seek it.

Max Lucado

~

Our Lord never drew power from Himself,
He drew it always from His Father.

Oswald Chambers

~

A mighty fortress is our God,
a bulwark never failing . . . .

Martin Luther

God will never lead you where
His strength cannot keep you.

Barbara Johnson

~

Measure the size of the obstacles
against the size of God.

Beth Moore

~

God's saints in all ages have realized
that God was enough for them.
God is enough for time;
God is enough for eternity.
God is enough!

Hannah Whitall Smith

We have ample evidence that the Lord
is able to guide. The promises cover every
imaginable situation. All we need to do
is to take the hand he stretches out.

Elisabeth Elliot

～

The Lord God of heaven and earth,
the Almighty Creator of all things, He who
holds the universe in His hand as though it
were a very little thing, He is your Shepherd,
and He has charged Himself with the care and
keeping of you, as a shepherd is charged
with the care and keeping of his sheep.

Hannah Whitall Smith

～

In God's faithfulness lies eternal security.

Corrie ten Boom

---

*I raise my eyes toward*
*the mountains.*
*Where will my help come from?*
*My help comes from the Lord,*
*the Maker of heaven and earth.*

—

Psalm 121:1-2 HCSB

---

# CHAPTER 15

# CELEBRATING CHRIST'S LOVE

*T*he inescapable promise of Christmas is this: Christ loves us. Even though we are imperfect, fallible beings, and even though we have fallen far short of God's commands, Christ's love is perfect and steadfast.

On the very first Christmas day, when God sent His Son to become the salvation of the world, He bestowed the ultimate gift, a gift that is beyond price and beyond human comprehension. We have not earned our salvation; even the best among us fall far short of God's commandments. But, when we accept Christ as our Savior, we are saved by God's grace.

As we celebrate His birth, let us accept Christ's love and share His Good News. Christ's love changes everything; may we, as believers, allow it to change everything in us.

We tend to focus our attention at Christmas
on the infancy of Christ. The greater truth
of the holiday is His deity. More astonishing
than a baby in the manger is the truth that
this promised baby is the omnipotent
Creator of the heavens and the earth!

John MacArthur

If you come to Christ, you will always have
the option of an ever-present friend.
You don't have to dial long-distance.
He'll be with you every step of the way.

Bill Hybels

*Greater love has no one than this,*
*than to lay down one's life for his friends.*

John 15:13 NKJV

Jesus:
the proof of God's love.

—

Philip Yancey

He loved us not because we're lovable,
but because He is love.

C. S. Lewis

The simple shepherds heard the voice of
an angel and found their Lamb;
the wise men saw the light of a star
and found their Wisdom.

Fulton Sheen

Our hope in Christ is the mainstream
of our joy.

C. H. Spurgeon

I truly believe that if we keep telling
the Christmas story, singing the Christmas
songs, and living the Christmas spirit,
we can bring joy and happiness
and peace to this world.

Norman Vincent Peale

Jesus stooped into an actual identification
with human nature, and, by that stoop,
lifted human nature into the spaciousness
of fellowship with God.

G. Campbell Morgan

The stunning point of Christmas is that God
considered my needs and the worth of my
relationship to Him to be sufficient cause to
go through the trauma of changing places.

Joe Stowell

*I am the door. If anyone enters by Me,*
*he will be saved.*
*I have come that they may have life,*
*and that they may have it more abundantly.*

John 10:9-10 NKJV

*I have come as a light into the world,*
*so that everyone who believes in Me*
*would not remain in darkness.*

John 12:46 HCSB

*At the name of Jesus every knee
should bow, of those in heaven,
and of those on earth,
and of those under the earth,
and that every tongue should
confess that Jesus Christ is Lord,
to the glory of God the Father.*

—

Philippians 2:10-11 NKJV

A believer comes to Christ;
a disciple follows after Him.

Vance Havner

Jesus Christ is not a security from storms.
He is perfect security in storms.

Kathy Troccoli

Being a Christian is more than just
an instantaneous conversion;
it is like a daily process whereby you grow
to be more and more like Christ.

Billy Graham

I have learned that the more we understand
how very much God loves us,
and the more we comprehend the grace
He has demonstrated toward us,
the more humble we become.

Serita Ann Jakes

A disciple is a follower of Christ.
That means you take on His priorities as
your own. His agenda becomes your agenda.
His mission becomes your mission.

Charles Stanley

Discipleship means personal,
passionate devotion to a Person,
our Lord Jesus Christ.

Oswald Chambers

Christ is not valued at all unless
He is valued above all.

St. Augustine

Begin to know Him now,
and finish never.

Oswald Chambers

The star of Bethlehem
was a star of joy.
"When they saw the star,
they rejoiced with
exceedingly great joy."
All true joy comes from Him.

—

D. James Kennedy

Love came down at Christmas,
Love all lovely, love divine;
Love was born at Christmas;
star and angels gave the sign.

—

Christina Rossetti

A Son of God who defends
his title with the arguments that he
is the brother of even the poorest
and the guilty and takes their
burden upon himself,
this is a fact one can only note and
shake one's head in unbelief,
or one must worship and adore.
There is no other alternative.
I must worship.
That's why I celebrate Christmas.

—

Helmut Thielicke

Everywhere, everywhere
Christmas tonight!
For the Christ child who comes
is the master of all;
No palace too great,
no cottage too small.

—

Phillips Brooks

*Who can separate us from the
love of Christ? Can affliction or
anguish or persecution
or famine or nakedness or danger
or sword? . . . No, in all these
things we are more than victorious
through Him who loved us.*

—

Romans 8:35, 37 HCSB

---

*"And they shall call His name*
*Immanuel,"*
*which is translated,*
*"God with us."*

—

Matthew 1:23 NKJV

---

# CHAPTER 16

# CELEBRATING THE GIFT OF ETERNAL LIFE

Two thousand years ago, God fulfilled His promise by sending His Son into this world so that those who open their hearts to Him might have eternal life. God has made His promise clear: When we accept God's Son and accept God's grace, we will receive life abundant and eternal. And that, of course, is God's ultimate Christmas gift to the world, a gift of love that is infinite, unshakable, unchanging, and eternal.

It is by God's grace that we have been saved, through faith. We are saved not because of our good deeds but because of our faith in Christ. May we, who have been given so much, praise our Savior for the gift of salvation, and may we share the joyous news of our Master's love and His grace.

*For the Son of Man has come to
seek and to save the lost.*

—

Luke 19:10 HCSB

*Jesus said to her, "I am the resurrection
and the life. The one who believes in Me,
even if he dies, will live. Everyone who lives and
believes in Me will never die—ever.
Do you believe this?"*

John 11:25-26 HCSB

*I have written these things to you who believe
in the name of the Son of God, so that you may
know that you have eternal life.*

1 John 5:13 HCSB

*Pursue righteousness, godliness, faith, love,
endurance, and gentleness. Fight the good fight
for the faith; take hold of eternal life,
to which you were called and have made a good
confession before many witnesses.*

1 Timothy 6:11-12 HCSB

Teach us to set our hopes on heaven,
to hold firmly to the promise of eternal life,
so that we can withstand the struggles and
storms of this world.

Max Lucado

And because we know Christ is alive,
we have hope for the present
and hope for life beyond the grave.

Billy Graham

God has promised us abundance, peace,
and eternal life. These treasures are ours for
the asking; all we must do is claim them. One
of the great mysteries of life is why on earth do
so many of us wait so very long
to lay claim to God's gifts?

Marie T. Freeman

Amazing Grace!
How sweet the sound that
saved a wretch like me!
I once was lost but now
am found; was blind,
but now I see.

—

John Newton

God did not spring forth from eternity;
He brought forth eternity.

C. H. Spurgeon

Slowly and surely, we learn the great secret
of life, which is to know God.

Oswald Chambers

Once a man is united to God,
how could he not live forever?
Once a man is separated from God,
what can he do but wither and die?

C. S. Lewis

Christ, the Son of God, the complete
embodiment of God's Word, came among us.
He looked on humanity's losing battle
with sin and pitched His divine tent
in the middle of the camp
so that He could dwell among us.

Beth Moore

Grace comes from the heart of a gracious
God who wants to stun you and overwhelm
you with a gift you don't deserve—salvation,
adoption, a spiritual ability to use in kingdom
service, answered prayer, the church,
His presence, His wisdom,
His guidance, His love.

Bill Hybels

I have been all over the world,
and I have never met anyone
who regretted giving
his or her life to Christ.

—

Billy Graham

MANY WITNESSES, ONE LORD

Also by William Barclay in this series

*The Apostles' Creed*
*At the Last Trumpet*
*Discovering Jesus*
*Good Tidings of Great Joy*
*Great Themes of the New Testament*
*Growing in Christian Faith*
*Letters to the Seven Churches*
*The Lord is My Shepherd*
*The Lord's Prayer*
*The Lord's Supper*
*The New Testament*
*New Testament Words*
*The Parables of Jesus*
*The Promise of the Spirit*
*The Ten Commandments*
*We Have Seen the Lord!*